MW00682401

High School Library
Peabody, Mass.

The World of Work

Choosing a Career in Nutrition

More and more people are becoming concerned with maintaining a healthy diet. This helps create jobs for those in the field of nutrition.

The World of Work
Choosing a Career in Nutrition

Sue Hurwitz

THE ROSEN PUBLISHING GROUP, INC.
NEW YORK

To GENE

For his unflagging interest in nutrition

Published in 1997, 1999 by The Rosen Publishing Group, Inc.
29 East 21st Street, New York, NY 10010

Copyright © 1997, 1999 by The Rosen Publishing Group, Inc.

Revised Edition 1999

All rights reserved. No part of this book may be reproduced in any form without permission in writing from the publisher, except by a reviewer.

Library of Congress Cataloging-in-Publication Data

Hurwitz, Sue, 1934–
      Choosing a career in nutrition / Sue Hurwitz.
            p.   cm.—(The world of work)
      Includes bibliographical references and index.
      Summary: Introduces various careers in the field of nutrition, including dietitians and doctors.
      ISBN 0-8239-3001-7
      1. Nutrition—Vocational guidance—Juvenile literature. [1. Dietitians—Vocational guidance. 2. Nutrition—Vocational guidance. 3. Vocational Guidance.] I. Title. II. Series: World of work (New York, NY)
TX357.H87 1996
363.8'023—dc20   96-9449
                                                                                CIP
                                                                                AC MN

Manufactured in the United States of America

Contents

Introduction

People are becoming more and more concerned about eating healthy foods. They are eager to learn how to make smart nutritional choices. They demand better foods and more detailed information on food labels.

Nutrition is the study of how food works inside the body. It is the science of a body's reaction to vitamins, minerals, fats, sugars, fiber, artificial chemicals, and all of the other elements that make up the food we eat. Career opportunities in nutrition are greater today than ever before. People who work in nutrition are found in many job settings.

Some people may go to school for many years and become scientists, doing experiments in laboratories with food substances and writing about what they find. This kind of work is a part of the field of nutrition. However, most people in nutrition have a very different type of job. They work in *nutritional care*, which is also called *dietetics*.

Sometimes, instead of the words "nutrition" and "nutritionist" you might hear or see the terms "dietetics" and "dietitian." Although it can be confusing, it is important to try to keep these terms straight.

Dietitians (people who practice dietetics) are the experts who learn about nutrient experiments conducted by scientists and use that knowledge to help people choose more healthful foods. Dietitians usually have a direct effect on how their clients eat.

To become a dietitian, you will need a bachelor's degree and you must pass state and federal board exams. A career in the dietetics branch of nutrition offers many opportunities. Registered dietitians plan menus in hospitals and nursing homes. They explain special diets to sick patients. They help people who have weight problems or allergies. They teach people to select and prepare nutritious foods. A registered dietitian can explain how wise food choices keep you healthy.

Dietetic technicians work under the guidance of registered dietitians. They may work in food service management, making sure an institution offers a balanced diet. Many school lunch programs are managed by a dietetic technician.

Some dietetic technicians work directly with people. They may give nutrition advice in a hospital. They may advise people at health spas or wellness centers. There are other kinds of dietitians as well. All of them are considered nutritionists.

The word *nutritionist* is not very specific. It can be used to refer to any kind of dietitian, to a biochemist in a laboratory, or even to a person who sells vitamins in a health food store. It simply means that the person works in some way with food as a source of nutrients for the body. Some health food stores and weight management clubs hire food counselors who call themselves "nutritionists." Because this word has no legal definition, people who use it don't need to have any special training. If you seek the advice of a nutritionist, be sure that person is registered with the *American Dietetic Association (ADA)*.

The ADA represents professional dietitians. (It does not represent people who work on the scientific end of nutrition.) The ADA was founded in 1917 during World War I, and has expanded greatly. Today, it has more than 65,000 members. Its most important function is to provide training standards that dietitians must meet in order to be approved by the ADA.

The ADA also provides information to the public about nutrition and can help people find registered dietitians in their own region.

This book focuses on careers in the dietetic branch of nutrition. Chapter five discusses how nutrition affects the work of some doctors and scientific researchers. However, most people who consider a career in nutrition want to work directly with people, to help them learn to eat a healthy diet. These professionals are dietitians.

Questions to Ask Yourself

Nutrition and dietetics are related but different. 1) What is the main difference between the two? 2) What do dietitians do? 3) What do nutritionists do?

As a dietician you get to work directly with the people who need your services.

Careers in Nutrition

1

Deciding which path to take in the field of nutrition depends upon many factors. If you want to work directly with clients and not have to go through many years of schooling, a career in dietetics may be for you.

Becky, Future Dietician

Becky's grandfather, Sol, had diabetes for many years. His body could not process sugar properly. When Becky was in tenth grade, her grandfather became very ill. Becky's grandmother tried to prepare the strict diet that Sol needed. But Sol often ate forbidden foods containing sugar. It became impossible to keep Sol on his diet.

Sol entered a hospital to bring his diabetes under control. Soon he lost his appetite. The amount of sugar in his bloodstream varied when he didn't eat properly. He began to lose weight. He needed to take more and more insulin to control his diabetes.

Becky often visited the hospital. She was there when the registered dietitian spoke with the family.

"Sol complains that he doesn't like the food on his tray," the dietitian reported. "But he won't tell us what he likes to eat."

"I know," Becky's grandmother replied. "When my husband doesn't feel well he can be grumpy."

"My dad doesn't care much for meat," Becky's mom added. "He likes pasta and tuna casseroles. He also likes fruit and soft foods."

Becky watched the dietitian take notes. She realized that the dietitian was trying to improve her grandfather's health. Becky saw how an improper diet worsened her grandfather's health. Would eating properly help him?

Becky noted that her grandfather's meals soon included macaroni and cheese, apple sauce, and peas. As Sol became happier with his meals, his appetite improved. His health started to improve too.

Becky understood the important role nutrition plays in health. She began to consider a career in dietetics.

"I'm going to ask the dietitian for an interview," Becky told her mom. "I want to

learn more about this profession. I may want to become a professional dietitian."

Becky spoke with the dietitian. The dietitian explained her duties as a clinical dietitian. She advised Becky to contact the ADA for more information.

"Working at a job gives a person insight into a career," the dietitian told Becky. "Would you like a volunteer job in the hospital's food service department? You can learn how we put together special diets."

"That would be great!" Becky agreed.

Dietetics also offers jobs outside of a hospital atmosphere, in other kinds of environments such as schools, nursing homes, or other institutions. Some people prefer that.

Dan, Future Dietetic Technician

When Dan was a little boy, he loved to watch his parents prepare meals in the kitchen. He loved to pretend that he was a chef in his own restaurant.

When Dan started elementary school, his interest in food grew. He often helped his mother or father with the cooking.

When Dan was in middle school, his mother worked full time. Dan prepared dinner every day after school to help out. He read cookbooks to find new recipes. He even created menus describing his nutritious meals. He really enjoyed running the kitchen.

In high school, Dan began to consider college. He made an appointment with his guidance counselor. Dan explained how important good nutrition was in his cooking. The counselor suggested that Dan write to the ADA for information about a career as a dietetic technician.

Dan read professional nutrition magazines at the library. The school counselor also advised him to take math, technical writing, and more computer classes. He was already taking biology, anatomy, and chemistry.

"These classes will give you a background for college," said Dan's adviser. "If you like these classes, you probably will enjoy a career in dietetics."

You, on the other hand, may have an extremely scientific mind and love to experiment. Or maybe you would like to become a doctor and wonder how the study of nutrition relates to that career. Both *scientific researchers* and *medical doctors* must hold advanced graduate degrees. You may be

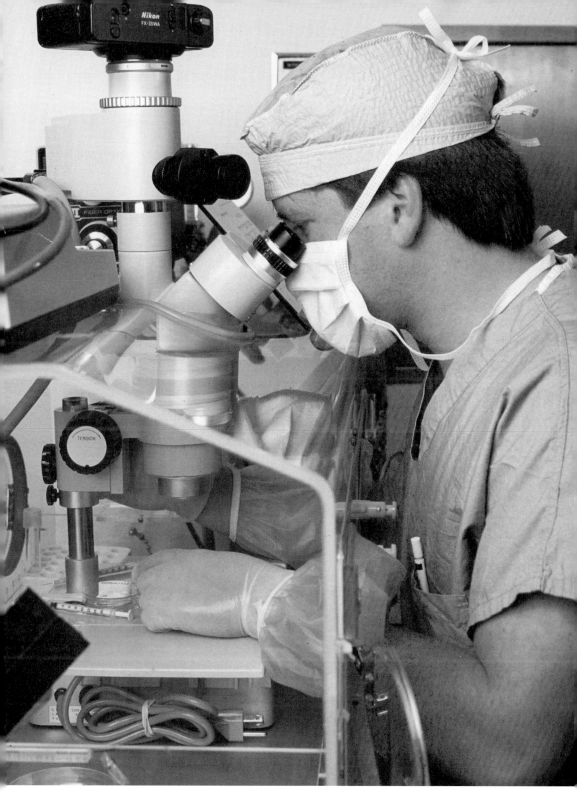

Some people are more interested in the scientific aspects of nutrition. Biochemistry is one field in which you can explore these aspects.

discouraged because of the cost of such an education. But, if you work hard, you may find that there are funds available from many sources to help you pay for school.

Nancy, Future Biochemist

Ever since she was in grade school, Nancy enjoyed her math and science classes. She especially liked microscopes. She used to stay after school sometimes to look at slides of cells. She always did her lab reports with great care. She would help describe her findings with neat charts and graphs.

One day her tenth-grade biology teacher, Mr. Jacobs, talked to her about how she might use her talents in the future. Nancy told Mr. Jacobs that she was interested in nutrition. He suggested that she take a biochemistry class. He explained that a career in biochemistry would let her do research on how nutrients are used in the body. She could discover why certain foods are more healthy than others. Mr. Jacobs said she might even help prevent diseases by studying which nutrients can keep people from getting sick.

Nancy was very excited to learn about this career. She took biochemistry and loved it. When it came time to apply for college, Nancy's guidance counselor helped her to apply for a science scholarship from the federal government. Nancy has been doing well in college, and she looks forward to getting a graduate degree in biochemistry.

Most people who work in nutrition decide not to pursue an advanced degree, at least not right away. Each of the young people described in this book works with nutrition for a different reason, and practices it in a different way.

Questions to Ask Yourself

Many interesting careers are available in nutrition and dietetics. 1) How was Becky's grandfather helped by a change in his diet? 2) How did Dan realize a childhood dream? 3) How will Nancy use her talents in math and science in the field of nutrition?

As a registered dietician, you need to be able to communicate well. You may need to work with a person's doctor to develop an appropriate diet for that person.

Preparing to Become a Dietitian

2

There are two categories in the field of dietetics: Registered Dietitian and Dietetic Technician, Registered. Each type has its own set of educational and professional requirements, set by the ADA.

Registered Dietitian

There are two ways to become a registered dietitian.

The plans differ depending on the college program you choose. Some programs are rated very highly by the ADA. They are called "ADA-accredited." This means that the bachelor's degree includes a lot of courses in nutrition and food science, as well as biology and psychology. An accredited program also offers the student a chance to try working with clients.

Some programs are considered acceptable by the ADA, but are not given its highest ranking. This category of college programs is called "ADA-approved." An approved program does not require any experience in the field as part of the bachelor's degree.

Plan 1. You can enroll in a college program *accredited* by the ADA. This leads to a four-year bachelor's degree. A nine- to twelve-month *internship* follows your bachelor's degree. An internship is on-the-job training.

Plan 2. You can earn a bachelor's degree in a program *approved* by the ADA. Afterward, you may need to complete supervised experience in the field. This experience must be in an approved Preprofessional Practice Program. It may also be in an accredited dietetic internship.

After completing either plan, you must take the Registration Examination for Dietitians. Your course work and internship prepare you for this exam. If you like, you can attend study sessions before taking it. The examination takes about four hours. Once you pass it, you become a *registered dietitian*. Then you can use the initials "R.D." after your name. This means that you are a food and nutrition expert.

Education Guidelines

Requirements for dietetics careers differ slightly from college to college. But all ADA programs require courses in the physical and biological sciences.

Sample basic classes include:

- anatomy
- biology
- biochemistry
- organic chemistry
- inorganic chemistry
- human physiology
- microbiology
- sociology or psychology
- economics
- anthropology or sociology

Depending on your choice of career, some classes in the following topics may also be needed:

- digesting and absorbing nutrients
- treating diseases through good nutrition
- food service
- math to intermediate algebra
- interviewing techniques
- purchasing and storing food
- diseases related to poor nutrition
- technical writing
- makeup of nutrients
- health care
- communication
- food preparation
- menu planning

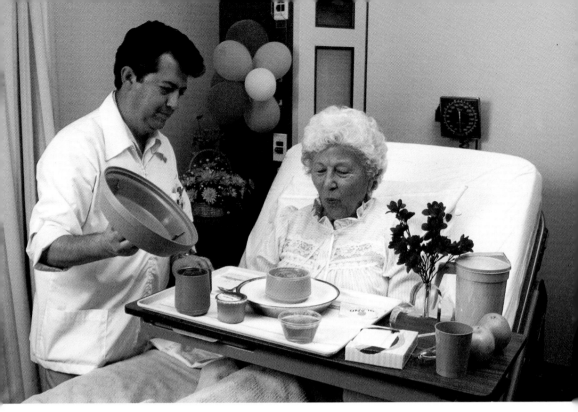

As a registered dietetic technician, you may work in a variety of settings, such as in a nursing home.

Classes explaining how the human body functions are obviously necessary. Dietetics professionals also need to understand people. Sociology and psychology classes help a person learn about human behavior.

As we saw with Becky's grandfather, ill people sometimes are difficult to treat. Dietitians need good communication skills when working with people. They also need patience and understanding.

Dietetic Technician, Registered
Becoming a dietetic technician, registered, requires less training than is needed to

become a registered dietitian. A person pursuing this career must earn a two-year associate degree in an ADA-approved program. This program combines classroom and supervised hands-on experience. About 450 hours of supervised experience is needed and can be in either nutrition care or food service management.

After getting the associate degree, you must take the Registration Examination for Dietetic Technicians. When you pass this exam you become a *dietetic technician*, *registered*, or D.T.R.

The ADA considers dietetic technicians, registered, to be assistants to registered dietetians.

The ADA requires that D.T.R.s earn fifty hours of continuing education every five years in order to keep working.

Educational Guidelines

D.T.R.s study normal nutrition. This includes how and why people eat, and how food works in the body. They study food digestion, absorption, and how the body receives energy from food. They learn about diet therapy for ill patients.

Many D.T.R.s work in the food service industry. To prepare for this they must study menu planning, food purchasing, and budgeting. They learn how to interpret food labels and food additives. They analyze rulings by the Food and Drug Administration, and study the way food is sanitized, processed, and packaged.

Before you decide to pursue training in dietetics, you should answer the following questions about yourself:

- Do you like to work in a team?
- Would you enjoy working with other health-care professionals?
- Do you like to plan and organize?
- Do you like to communicate?
- Do you enjoy gathering information and organizing it?
- Are you good in math and English?
- Are you a good listener?
- Would you like working on a computer?

If you answered "yes" to many of these questions, you may make a great dietitian. The above personality traits and skills are helpful for careers in nutritional care. Dietetics professionals work in many different settings.

Your interests and personality traits are important in finding the right career for you.

Questions to Ask Yourself

Dietitians may be trained in two different ways. 1) What is the difference between ADA-accredited and ADA-approved programs? 2) Which program requires supervised experience? 3) Who assists a registered dietitian?

Clinical dieticians evaluate and determine a patient's nutritional needs.

Registered Dietitian: Lots of Opportunities 3

Registered dietitians work in a variety of job settings. This chapter explores some of the opportunities available to R.D.s.

Clinical Dietitians

Clinical dietitians are registered dietitians who often work as part of a medical team. They may work in hospitals, nursing homes, and other health-care centers. They help speed a patient's recovery. They also help create long-term health plans by teaching patients how to follow special diets.

Clinical dietitians evaluate patients' needs. Sometimes they manage the food service department in their institution. They do research and use it to update their skills and knowledge.

Clinical dietitians often specialize in certain areas. Pediatrics, heart disease, and diabetes are three common areas of specialty.

Specialists usually have at least a master's degree.

Clinical dietitians who become part of a medical team generally have more medical and psychological training than other R.D.s. They may weigh patients, take blood pressure and order necessary lab tests.

An average beginning yearly salary in a hospital for a clinical R.D. with a bachelor's degree is about $22,000.

Jega, Clinical R.D.

Jega lives in Walla Walla, Washington. He always knew that he wanted to have a health-related career. His high school counselor suggested looking into the field of dietetics (the science of applying the principles of nutrition to the diet). Jega met with dietitians in various nursing homes and hospitals and then wrote to the American Dietetic Association (ADA) for more information.

Jega enrolled in a college with a four-year ADA-approved program. After college he completed a one-year internship in long-term patient care. He now works with a team of health care professionals. They treat long-term patients with nutritional problems.

Jega loves contributing to the health and happiness of his patients. He also likes being part of a medical team because they work well together and learn a lot from each other. Jega hopes to eventually earn a master's degree and specialize in pediatric care.

Community Dietitians

Community dietitians are registered dietitians who typically work for government health programs. They also work for agencies and businesses in their local communities. They teach people about food and good nutrition through the medium of public health programs. Some community dietitians develop food plans for families with low incomes. They advise single parents and senior citizens about healthy diets. They may also work at day care centers.

Justin, Community R.D.

Justin is a registered dietitian for a community program paid for by the federal government. In Tucson, Arizona, Justin works with several dietetic technicians who help with projects.

Community dietitians may help develop the menus for a program such as Project Open Hand. Project Open Hand serves nutritious meals to people who have HIV or AIDS.

Justin shows senior citizens how to prepare nutritious meals. He and the D.T.R.s teach the disabled about healthy food choices. Part of his job is to organize an outreach program that delivers hot meals to people who cannot leave their homes due to illness.

Justin must create different kinds of meals and keep the cost of the meals within a certain budget. Then he must find volunteers to deliver the meals. He must plan well and stay organized. His computer and business skills are a great help in his career.

Consultant Dietitians

Consultant dietitians are self-employed registered dietitians. They work freelance, either full-time or part-time. Some work with food companies, others with clinics or nursing homes.

They often are hired by athletes or health clubs to give advice about healthy diets. They evaluate their own clients' needs. Some of their clients are referred to them by doctors.

Olivia, Consultant R.D.

Olivia worked as a clinical R.D. in a hospital for five years. Then she started her own consulting business. Her first two clients were referred to her by doctors. Both clients had high cholesterol levels in their bodies. High cholesterol can lead to serious health problems. To lower their cholesterol levels, they needed to change their eating habits. Olivia counseled them on food choices and monitored their progress.

Olivia soon contacted a large business corporation. She asked about the wellness program for their employees. She discovered they had a fitness program but no nutrition counseling. The corporation asked her to write a proposal explaining her services.

Olivia's proposal included group dietary education sessions. She suggested sign-ups for luncheons featuring nutritious foods. She proposed more nutritious food choices in the company cafeteria. She wrote a sample newsletter with nutrition information. She suggested that employees could consult her privately to discuss their diets.

The company believed a wellness program would benefit their employees. The program could help cut down health-related absences. They hired Olivia on a permanent part-time basis.

Olivia also became a consultant for a national weight loss center. She trained salespeople from the center's local clinics. She explained basic nutrition and showed them how to take a client's history. Olivia designed menus and recipes suited to a client's food preferences.

Business/Industry Dietitians

Business/industry dietitians are registered dietitians who work in nutrition and food-related industries. They often include marketing and sales classes in their schooling. They may develop and test new nutrition products and foods. They may sell these

Exercise and good nutrition are both necessary to keep your body healthy.

One way to teach people good nutrition is by actually showing them ways to cook healthy meals.

products for their companies. They often work to develop positive public relations.

Maria, Business/Industry R.D.

Maria always planned to go into sales. She enjoyed talking with people. She liked the challenge of selling things. But Maria also wanted the stability of a career in nutrition. So she combined both her interests.

While in college, Maria took many business courses. She found that she liked the field of public relations. After graduating Maria found a job with a major fast-food corporation. She trained in their food lab for a year working with other R.D.s. They hoped to develop new products besides the company's sandwiches.

Then Maria was promoted to the public relations department. She wrote flyers describing the nutritional values of their products. She traveled to many of the company stores to improve employee knowledge about the products. She spoke with vendors about the nutritional content of their products. She discussed her company's products with large corporations who installed on-site food operations.

Maria found her career rewarding. She enjoyed her duties. She felt she did a good job of representing her company.

Educator Dietitians

Educator dietitians are registered dietitians who usually have a graduate degree. They teach the science of food and nutrition in colleges, universities, and technical schools. Their students include future nurses, doctors, dietitians, and dietetic technicians.

Stephen, Educator

When Stephen was in high school, he considered going into medicine. After his junior year, he started a volunteer job at a hospital. He helped move people from admissions to their rooms.

Stephen watched R.D.s help feed long-term care patients through tubes. He realized that R.D.s are an important part of a medical team. Stephen decided to become a registered dietitian.

Stephen planned to go into nutrition education. He didn't enjoy the clinical setting of a hospital. But he loved a school atmosphere. He knew he could feel fulfilled by teaching at the college level.

So Stephen studied hard and earned a Ph.D. degree in nutrition. He took an ADA-approved internship for one year and passed the ADA exam.

Today, Stephen teaches future doctors, nurses, R.D.s, and D.T.R.s. He feels his career makes a valuable contribution to the field of health care.

Research Dietitians

Research dietitians typically have a graduate degree. They are registered dietitians who make dietary recommendations resulting from testing foods. They may conduct nutritional experiments and search for alternative foods.

Research dietitians often work for food and pharmaceutical companies. Some work in universities or medical centers, or for the government.

Casey, Research R.D.

Casey earned a Master of Science degree in nutrition. She was interested in what U.S. soldiers ate during war. She noticed that service personnel were often given their food in powdered, or dehydrated, form. Dehydrating the food kept it from spoiling.

After she received her degree, Casey got a job in nutritional research for the U.S. government, improving the taste of dehydrated meals.

The federal government provides dehydrated meals for the homeless, the military, and for space personnel. Casey hopes her work may help improve the texture and taste of nutritious dehydrated meals.

Travis, Research R.D.

Travis always enjoyed chemistry. In high school, he began thinking about pursuing a career in research dietetics. Travis' parents advised him to talk with his school counselor.

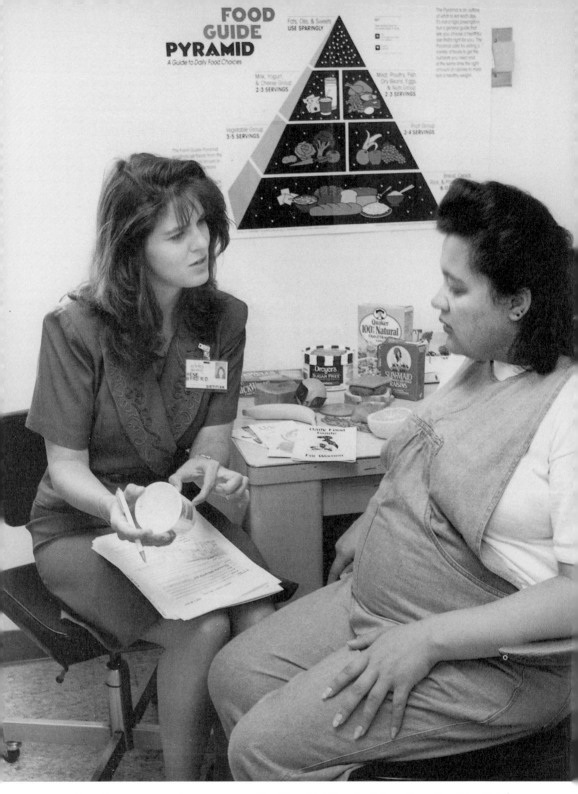

Sometimes pregnant women consult with a dietitian to determine a healthy diet for themselves and their growing baby.

His counselor said that work experience would be a great way to find out if he would like a job in this field. She advised Travis to visit their local cupcake company to ask about an internship.

The local company was happy to offer Travis an internship. Travis soon knew that he would enjoy a career in research helping to create more nutritious snacks. He wrote to the ADA for information on careers in dietetics. He wrote to colleges for catalogs of their classes.

After Travis earned his M.S., R.D. degree he took a nine-month internship with a bakery in an ADA-approved program. Then he took a three-month internship with the local cupcake company.

The local company offered Travis a job. He is now researching how to add nutrients into a new line of snack cakes. Travis is very happy with his career.

Management/Administrative Dietitians

Management/administrative dietitians oversee food service systems. They may manage the food service department of large companies. They may work in hospitals, nursing homes, schools, or restaurants.

These registered dietitians plan healthy meals and menus. They monitor food purchases, inventory, and budgets. They also supervise dietetic technicians and assistants.

Shana, Management/Administrative R.D.

I work for a health spa. We cater to clients who want to lose weight. I control the food service department. I manage the food service personnel, including two D.T.R.s who help me. I select and order all food and beverages and design nutritious meals within a certain budget. I vary the menus, keeping them low in calories and tasting good.

I prepared for my career by taking science, psychology, health, and nutrition classes in high school. I enrolled in an ADA-approved four-year course in college. There I took classes in marketing, public relations, accounting, and writing. I knew that a well-rounded nutrition background would help me find a job. I followed my degree with an ADA-approved internship for one year and then took the ADA exam.

I am very satisfied with my career. I feel that I make a difference in our clients' lives. When our clients leave here, many of them thank me.

They appreciate the nutritious meals and they plan to follow up with them at home.

Salaries
- As of 1998, the average salary for registered dietitians with one to five years of experience was from $30,000 to $35,000 per year.
- R.D.s with six to ten years of experience earn between $35,000 and $40,000 per year.
- All of these salaries are based on a full-time workweek of thirty-one hours or more. These facts were reported by the ADA research services.

R.D.s with M.S. and Ph.D degrees earned higher salaries. Salaries vary geographically; the classified ad section of the Journal of the ADA provides current salary information by region.

Questions to Ask Yourself
Dietitians can work in many different kinds of jobs. 1) List the duties of a clinical R.D. 2) How do community dietitians improve the quality of life for people in the area? 3) Where might a research dietitian work?

A D.T.R. may work with an R.D. to help determine what foods should be
included in a school lunch program.

Dietetic Technicians, Registered, At Work

4

Dietetic Technician, Registered

Dietetic technicians also work in many settings. Like registered dietitians, D.T.R.s also may specialize in certain areas. They may also work directly under the supervision of an R.D. such as in the following areas:

- Clinical Psychiatrics
- Pediatric Practice
- Critical Care

Each of these speciality fields requires additional training.

Dietetic technicians, registered, often work with R.D.s in hospitals and nursing homes. They may work in public health nutrition programs and school lunch programs.

D.T.R.s work in health clubs and for community wellness centers. Some work in nutrition programs for the elderly. They may

Dietitians who work in health clubs stress the importance of drinking enough water during and after your workout.

also work for food companies, often working in food service management settings.

D.T.R.s develop recipes, purchase food, and supervise inventory. They screen patients to find nutrition problems and keep track of their progress. In addition, they provide counseling and education to certain groups or individuals.

Ilya, Health Club D.T.R.

When Ilya was little, he liked to read books about skaters, swimmers, and skiers. When he was older, he knew that he would have a

sports-related career. His father, Gregor
Poprovnic, had been a famous gymnast in
the Soviet Union. When Mr. Poprovnic
moved to the United States, he and his wife
decided that they would raise their children
in an environment that stressed the
importance of athletics, nutrition, and
health. In his third year of high school, Ilya
discussed different career options with his
guidance counselor at school.

Ilya's counselor, Miss Reyes, advised him
to take courses in anatomy, nutrition,
business, and psychology. These classes
would provide Ilya with a broad enough
background to work in any health-related
field. Miss Reyes also suggested that Ilya
contact the American Dietetic Association
for information about a career as a dietetic
technician.

Ilya worked hard in school, and as a
result the ADA awarded him a scholarship.
He earned an associate's degree and passed
the Registration Examination for Dietetic
Technicians.

Ilya is now a health club D.T.R. He
advises clients on which foods they should
eat in order to perform better and feel
healthy. Ilya teaches them about the

importance of eating carbohydrates for energy, especially the morning of and the night before a big workout. He also works with a registered dietitian twice a week to implement a diet regimen. Since health and nutrition have always been important to Ilya, he is lucky to have found a way to combine his interests with his career.

Ilya's parents are very pleased that their son is doing work that he likes. They have seen many young people suffer because they were unable to find a career doing something that they really cared about.

Mary, School Lunch Program D.T.R.

Mary works under the supervision of an R.D. in a large school district. It is her job to supervise the personnel and food service for three high schools. She also purchases food and keeps records of it on a computer.

Mary spends one day in each of her schools on a rotating basis. She discusses menus, food preparation, and sanitation with her cooks. Every two weeks she reports to her supervising R.D.

Mary feels that she helps the students who eat lunch in her schools. She finds her work both challenging and interesting.

Community D.T.R.s counsel a variety of people in their community on the foods that make up a healthy diet.

Kelsey, Community D.T.R.

My parents always stressed the importance of eating "right." I realize there is a connection between diet and health and disease.

Pictures of starving children on TV often made me wish I could help them or others like them. When I began thinking of a career, I naturally investigated careers in nutrition.

I work with an R.D. for a state wellness program called WIC. *The initials stand for Women, Infants and Children.* WIC *provides food and nutrition counseling to poor or pregnant women and their young children.* WIC *now has been expanded to include working families who meet federal income guidelines.*

I rarely see clients as poorly nourished as children shown on TV. Yet many of our clients don't get enough nourishing food. Some don't even know what foods are nutritious. They may not know how to prepare foods properly.

I provide nutritious foods for sample meals. I explain nutritious recipes. I educate clients about the five food groups from which we should eat in order to have a balanced diet. I stress the importance of limiting fats, oils, and sugary foods.

I also counsel the elderly about nutritious diets. Many elderly people live alone on fixed incomes. I often go to their homes to teach them how to make wiser food choices.

I am very happy with my career. I enjoy talking with my clients, and I feel that I help improve their lives and health. It's nice to make a difference in someone's life.

Salaries

As of 1998, the average salary for D.T.R.s with one to five years of experience was between $20,000 and $25,000 per year. D.T.R.s with six to ten years of experience earn between $25,000 and $30,000 per year. These salaries are based on a full-time workweek of thirty-one hours of more.

The average salary for a dietetic technician, registered, varies from region to region. Salaries can also vary with the amount of responsibility. The classified ad section of the *Journal of the* ADA provides current regional salary information.

Questions to Ask Yourself

The dietetic technician, registered, has the option to work in many settings, each requiring additional training. 1) Would you enjoy working in a health club? 2) Do you think that a school-lunch program D.T.R. offers a useful service? 3) Would you prefer working with the younger or older residents of a community?

Doctors and the Field of Nutrition

5

Because nutrition and health are so closely related, you might think that a person could become a medical doctor specializing in nutrition. This is not quite the way it works.

All students in medical school take basic courses in nutrition and biochemistry. They then go on to a certain branch of medicine, for instance pediatrics—working with children, internal medicine—general medicine, or surgery. Nutrition is important in every one of these branches. But most physicians do not specialize in nutrition. So they depend on the registered dietitians on their hospital staff to work with them on nutrition programs for their patients. As you have seen, some R.D.s get a master's degree in a specialty area such as pediatrics. That way, they are qualified to assist a doctor in this field.

The ADA encourages doctors to learn more about nutrition. It also encourages physicians

If you are interested in a career in the field of nutrition, you can find out more about the specific jobs at your local library.

to consult R.D.s whenever the diet of a patient must be altered.

In the last decade or so it has become more common for physicians to get extra training in nutrition. Usually they do this through a *clinical nutrition program.* These programs are offered at about fifty universities throughout the United States. They are one- to three-year training programs intended for people who already have an advanced medical degree. Usually a university or hospital provides a grant so that a doctor can participate in a clinical nutrition program. For example, the ADA recommends the American College of Nutrition in Scarsdale, New York.

Other Careers in Nutrition

Although people do not often get an M.D. in nutrition, it is common to earn a Ph.D. in nutritional science, biochemistry, or another related field. People who choose to do this often *teach* nutrition or do *research.*

There are many kinds of research that can be done in nutrition. Not everything can be used directly by dietitians to improve their clients' diets. The study of nutrition intersects with many other fields of interest. Here are a few examples of the type of research that is done in nutrition at the Ph.D. level:

- The relationship between certain nutrients and the risk of cancer.
- How diet can reduce the risk of a sports or dance injury.
- How diet changes can help alcoholics or drug addicts.
- How nutrition affects the quality of life of the elderly.
- The effects of chemicals added to foods to preserve them.
- How nutrition affects school performance and the behavior of children.
- The relationship between nutrients and the immune system, the way our bodies fight illness.
- How feeding certain nutrients to livestock affects the flavor and quality of meat.
- Methods of drying and preserving food.
- The history and dietary customs of different cultures.
- What people ate thousands of years ago.
- Why people prefer certain foods.
- What foods we should feed our pets for a healthy life.

Each of these topics requires a certain area of expertise. Yet all of them deal with how the substances in food react in a living body. This is the science of nutrition.

Questions to Ask Yourself

Medical doctors operate in separate fields from nutritionists. The ADA encourages greater cooperation between the two. 1) Would you like to do research in nutrition? 2) What area of research do you find interesting? Why?

Classes such as biology and chemistry can help prepare you for a career in nutrition.

Getting Started 6

Taking control of your future career is important. Consider your interests and skills. Think about the type of work that seems challenging. Begin preparing for that goal now. You may decide that a career in nutrition is something you want to explore.

If you are still in high school, take classes in the physical and biological sciences. Take other classes suggested in chapter one. Discuss your ideas with your parents or school counselor. Talk with people working in the field. See if you can get experience through *volunteering*—working with someone in the field of nutrition for no pay.

Collect information to help with your decision. Read about careers in nutrition. Contact the American Dietetic Association or the American College of Nutrition for information. Write to colleges and ask for catalogs describing their nutrition or biochemistry programs.

Think about the various types of nutrition careers. Do your interests, skills, and personality traits seem suited to a dietetic career? Perhaps you would rather work in the biological sciences. Consider what level of education you might want to pursue.

Your future is in your own hands. Plan for it! Prepare for it! Enjoy it!

Questions to Ask Yourself

Your future is in your hands. It's never too soon to begin considering it. 1) What classes can you take to help prepare you for a career in nutrition? 2) Could information from the ADA and colleges help you make up your mind? 3) How can you obtain that information?

Glossary

American Dietetic Association (ADA) Professional organization of dietitians and nutritionists.

cholesterol Soft, waxy fat that circulates in the blood.

dietetics Science of how food affects one's health.

dietary technician, registered Food expert with a two-year associate degree and an ADA-approved internship, who has passed an ADA exam.

food service system Various activities of planning nutritious menus, preparing food, and serving meals.

internship On-the-job training.

malnutrition Imbalance of nutrients due to lack of food or disease.

metabolism Rate at which a person burns calories.

nutrients Vitamins and minerals essential to good health.

nutrition   Science of food and how your body uses food.

registered dietitian   Food expert who has at least a four-year bachelor's degree from an ADA-accredited or approved program, an ADA-approved internship, and has passed an ADA exam.

For Further Reading

Cooper, Kenneth H. *Advanced Nutritional Therapies*. Nashville, TN: Thomas Nelson Publishers, 1998.

Heyer, Albrecht A., Earl R. Mindell, and Richard A. Passwater (eds.). *Beginners Introduction to Nutrition: The Simple Facts to Help Achieve and Maintain Good Health*. New Canaan, CT: Keats Publishing, 1996.

Hopkins, Edward J. *Career Options in Healthcare*. Gaithersburg, MD: Aspen Publishers, 1998.

Ronzio, Robert. *Encyclopedia of Nutrition and Good Health*. New York: Facts on File, 1997.

Wilson, Robert F. *Your Career in Nutrition*. Happague, NY: Barrons Educational Series, 1996.

For More Information

In the United States

American College of Nutrition
c/o Hospital for Joint Disease
301 East 17th Street
New York, NY 10003
(212)777-1037

American Dietetic Association
216 West Jackson Boulevard
Chicago, IL 60606-6996
(800) 877-1600
web site:
  http://www.eatright.org

Commission on
  Accreditation/Approval for
  Dietetic Education
American Dietetic Association
216 West Jackson Boulevard
Chicago, IL 60606-6996
(312) 899-0040, ext. 5400
web site:
  http://www.eatright.org/caade
Provides information for those
  interested in pursuing a
  career in nutrition

In Canada

Dietitians of Canada
480 University Avenue, Suite
  604
Toronto, Ontario M5G 1V2
(416) 596-0857
web site:
  http://dietitians.ca

Food Institute of Canada
415-1600 Scott Street
Ottawa, Ontario K1Y 4N7
(613) 722-1000
web site:
  http://www.foodnet.fic.ca

Health Canada
A.L. 0913A
Ottawa, Ontario K1A 0K9
(613) 957-2991
web sites:
  http://www.hc-sc.gc.ca/
  english
  http://www.hc-sc.gc.ca/
  francais

Ordre Professionel des
  Diététistes du Québec
1425, Boulevard René-
  Lévesque Ouest, Salle 703
Montréal, Québec H3G 1T7
(415) 393-3733
web site: http://www.opdq.org

Foodlines
contains archive of culinary tips
  and healthy eating section
http:// www.foodlines.com

**List of Canadian universities
offering Dietitians of
Canada accredited
programs in dietetic
education:**

Ryerson Polytechnic University
School of Nutrition, Consumer,
  and Family Studies
350 Victoria Street
Toronto, Ontario M5N 2N8
(416) 979-5000, ext. 7072

University of British Columbia
  School of Family and
  Nutritional Sciences
2205 East Mall
Vancouver, British Columbia
V6T 1Z4
(604) 822-6869

Index

About the Author

Sue Hurwitz earned an M.A. in education from the University of Missouri, She spent many years in the classroom and taught grades K through 9.

Ms. Hurwitz is the author/coauthor of fourteen books, including: *Staying Healthy, Coping with Homelessness, Careers Inside the World of Entrepreneurs, Careers Inside the World of Government*, and *Choosing a Career in Film, Television, or Video*.

Photo Credits

Cover © Scott Stallard/Image Bank; p. 2 © Peter Kelly/Impact Visuals; p. 10 © Rick Gerharter/Impact Visuals; p. 15 © Paul S. Howell/Gamma Liaison; p. 18 © Bruce Wodoler/Image Bank; p. 22 © Vladimir Lange/Image Bank; p. 33 by Michael Brandt; p. 34 © Allan Clear/Impact Visuals; p. 38 © Alain McLaughlin/Impact Visuals; p. 42 © Brian Palmer/Impact Visuals; p. 44 © Ken Huang/Image Bank; p. 47 © F.M. Kearney/Impact Visuals; p. 52 by Katherine Hsu, p. 56 © Ansell Horn/Impact Visuals;